# THE BEATLES

## BELLS / GLOCKENSPIEL

ISBN 978-1-70512-157-3

Visit Hal Leonard Online at
**www.halleonard.com**

Contact us:
**Hal Leonard**
7777 West Bluemound Road
Milwaukee, WI 53213
Email: info@halleonard.com

In Europe, contact:
**Hal Leonard Europe Limited**
42 Wigmore Street
Marylebone, London, W1U 2RN
Email: info@halleonardeurope.com

In Australia, contact:
**Hal Leonard Australia Pty. Ltd.**
4 Lentara Court
Cheltenham, Victoria, 3192 Australia
Email: info@halleonard.com.au

# ACROSS THE UNIVERSE

BELLS

Words and Music by JOHN LENNON
and PAUL McCARTNEY

# ALL MY LOVING

Bells

Words and Music by JOHN LENNON
and PAUL McCARTNEY

# ALL YOU NEED IS LOVE

BELLS

Words and Music by JOHN LENNON
and PAUL McCARTNEY

# AND I LOVE HER

BELLS

Words and Music by JOHN LENNON
and PAUL McCARTNEY

# BACK IN THE U.S.S.R.

BELLS

Words and Music by JOHN LENNON
and PAUL McCARTNEY

# BLACKBIRD

BELLS

Words and Music by JOHN LENNON
and PAUL McCARTNEY

# CAN'T BUY ME LOVE

Words and Music by JOHN LENNON
and PAUL McCARTNEY

BELLS

# CARRY THAT WEIGHT

BELLS

Words and Music by JOHN LENNON
and PAUL McCARTNEY

# COME TOGETHER

BELLS

Words and Music by JOHN LENNON
and PAUL McCARTNEY

# DAY TRIPPER

BELLS

Words and Music by JOHN LENNON
and PAUL McCARTNEY

# DO YOU WANT TO KNOW A SECRET?

BELLS

Words and Music by JOHN LENNON
and PAUL McCARTNEY

# EIGHT DAYS A WEEK

BELLS

Words and Music by JOHN LENNON
and PAUL McCARTNEY

# ELEANOR RIGBY

Words and Music by JOHN LENNON
and PAUL McCARTNEY

BELLS

# THE FOOL ON THE HILL

BELLS

Words and Music by JOHN LENNON
and PAUL McCARTNEY

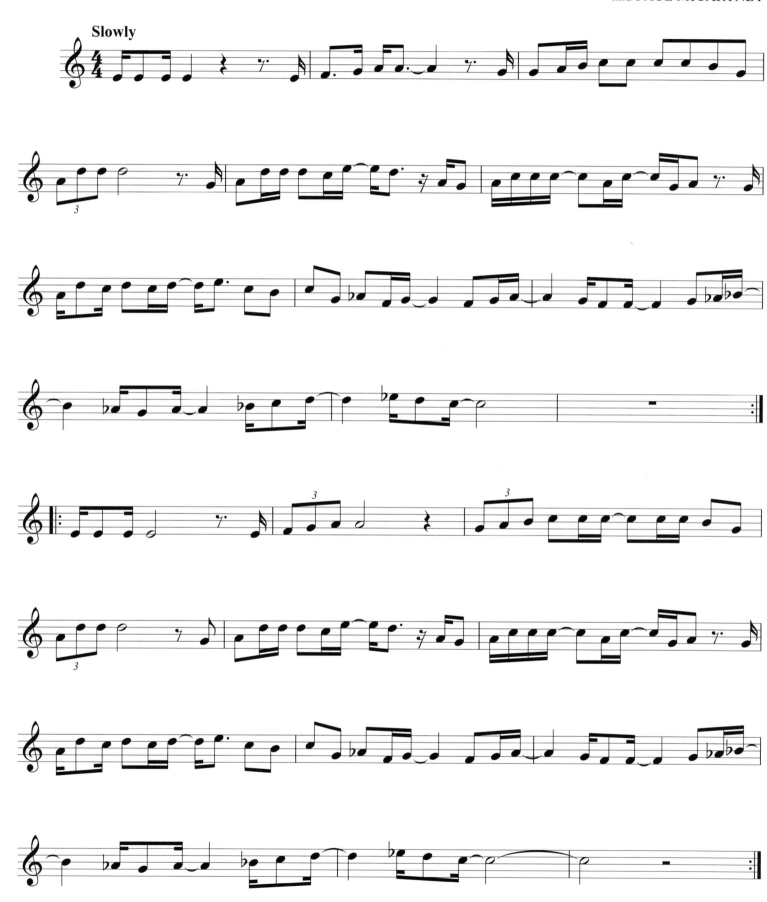

# FROM ME TO YOU

BELLS

Words and Music by JOHN LENNON
and PAUL McCARTNEY

# GET BACK

BELLS

Words and Music by JOHN LENNON
and PAUL McCARTNEY

# GIRL

BELLS

Words and Music by JOHN LENNON
and PAUL McCARTNEY

**Easy lilting beat**

# GOLDEN SLUMBERS

BELLS

Words and Music by JOHN LENNON
and PAUL McCARTNEY

# GOOD DAY SUNSHINE

BELLS

Words and Music by JOHN LENNON
and PAUL McCARTNEY

# GOT TO GET YOU INTO MY LIFE

Bells

Words and Music by JOHN LENNON
and PAUL McCARTNEY

# A HARD DAY'S NIGHT

Words and Music by JOHN LENNON
and PAUL McCARTNEY

Bells

# HELLO, GOODBYE

BELLS

Words and Music by JOHN LENNON
and PAUL McCARTNEY

# HELP!

Words and Music by JOHN LENNON
and PAUL McCARTNEY

BELLS

# HERE COMES THE SUN

BELLS

Words and Music by
GEORGE HARRISON

# HERE, THERE AND EVERYWHERE

BELLS

Words and Music by JOHN LENNON
and PAUL McCARTNEY

**Moderately slow**

# HEY JUDE

BELLS

Words and Music by JOHN LENNON
and PAUL McCARTNEY

# I FEEL FINE

BELLS

Words and Music by JOHN LENNON
and PAUL McCARTNEY

**Bright Rock**

# I SAW HER STANDING THERE

Bells

Words and Music by JOHN LENNON
and PAUL McCARTNEY

# I SHOULD HAVE KNOWN BETTER

BELLS

Words and Music by JOHN LENNON
and PAUL McCARTNEY

# I WANT TO HOLD YOUR HAND

Bells

Words and Music by JOHN LENNON
PAUL McCARTNEY

Moderately, with a beat

# I WILL

BELLS

Words and Music by JOHN LENNON
and PAUL McCARTNEY

**Moderately**

# I'LL FOLLOW THE SUN

BELLS

Words and Music by JOHN LENNON
and PAUL McCARTNEY

# IF I FELL

Words and Music by JOHN LENNON
and PAUL McCARTNEY

Bells

# IN MY LIFE

Bells

Words and Music by JOHN LENNON
and PAUL McCARTNEY

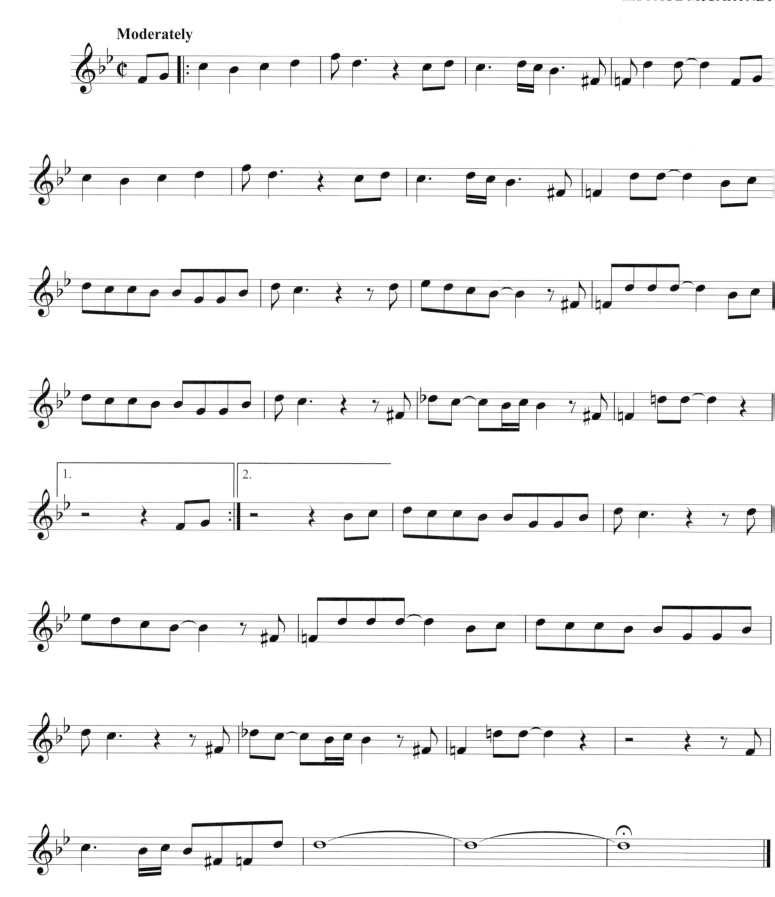

# LADY MADONNA

BELLS

Words and Music by JOHN LENNON
and PAUL McCARTNEY

# LET IT BE

BELLS

Words and Music by JOHN LENNON
PAUL McCARTNEY

# THE LONG AND WINDING ROAD

BELLS

Words and Music by JOHN LENNON
and PAUL McCARTNEY

# LOVE ME DO

Bells

Words and Music by JOHN LENNON<br/>and PAUL McCARTNEY

# LUCY IN THE SKY WITH DIAMONDS

BELLS

Words and Music by JOHN LENNON
and PAUL McCARTNEY

# MAGICAL MYSTERY TOUR

BELLS

Words and Music by JOHN LENNON
and PAUL McCARTNEY

# MICHELLE

BELLS

Words and Music by JOHN LENNON
and PAUL McCARTNEY

# NORWEGIAN WOOD
## (This Bird Has Flown)

BELLS

Words and Music by JOHN LENNON
and PAUL McCARTNEY

# NOWHERE MAN

BELLS

Words and Music by JOHN LENNON
and PAUL McCARTNEY

# OB-LA-DI, OB-LA-DA

Bells

Words and Music by JOHN LENNON
and PAUL McCARTNEY

# OCTOPUS'S GARDEN

BELLS

Words and Music by
RICHARD STARKEY

**Moderately bright, in 2**

# PAPERBACK WRITER

Words and Music by JOHN LENNON
and PAUL McCARTNEY

**Bright Rock**

# PENNY LANE

Words and Music by JOHN LENNON
and PAUL McCARTNEY

BELLS

# REVOLUTION

Bells

Words and Music by JOHN LENNON
and PAUL McCARTNEY

# SHE LOVES YOU

Words and Music by JOHN LENNON
and PAUL McCARTNEY

BELLS

# SOMETHING

BELLS

Words and Music by
GEORGE HARRISON

# STRAWBERRY FIELDS FOREVER

BELLS

Words and Music by JOHN LENNON
and PAUL McCARTNEY

# TICKET TO RIDE

BELLS

Words and Music by JOHN LENNON
and PAUL McCARTNEY

# TWIST AND SHOUT

BELLS

Words and Music by BERT RUSSELL
and PHIL MEDLEY

# WE CAN WORK IT OUT

**Bells**

Words and Music by JOHN LENNON
and PAUL McCARTNEY

# WHEN I'M SIXTY-FOUR

ELLS

Words and Music by JOHN LENNON
and PAUL McCARTNEY

# WHILE MY GUITAR GENTLY WEEPS

BELLS

Words and Music by
GEORGE HARRISON

# WITH A LITTLE HELP FROM MY FRIENDS

BELLS

Words and Music by JOHN LENNON
and PAUL McCARTNEY

# YELLOW SUBMARINE

BELLS

Words and Music by JOHN LENNON
and PAUL McCARTNEY

# YESTERDAY

BELLS

Words and Music by JOHN LENNON
and PAUL McCARTNEY

# YOU'VE GOT TO HIDE YOUR LOVE AWAY

Bells

Words and Music by JOHN LENNON
and PAUL McCARTNEY